19/53

THE
DIVERTING HISTORY OF
JOHN GILPIN

SHOWING HOW HE WENT FARTHER
THAN HE INTENDED AND CAME
SAFE HOME AGAIN

BY

WILLIAM COWPER

———•◦•———

WITH MANY ILLUSTRATIONS BY

RONALD SEARLE

———•◦•———

LONDON
PENGUIN BOOKS
1953

THE KING PENGUIN BOOKS

EDITOR: N. B. L. PEVSNER · TECHNICAL EDITOR: R. B. FISHENDEN

PUBLISHED BY PENGUIN BOOKS LTD

HARMONDSWORTH, MIDDLESEX, ENGLAND

PENGUIN BOOKS INC, 3300 CLIPPER MILL ROAD

BALTIMORE, MARYLAND, U.S.A.

PENGUIN BOOKS PTY LTD, 200 NORMANBY ROAD

MELBOURNE, AUSTRALIA

THIS BOOK
FIRST PUBLISHED
1953

MADE AND PRINTED IN GREAT BRITAIN BY
HARRISON AND SONS LTD, LONDON

JOHN GILPIN was a citizen
    Of credit and renown,
A train-band captain eke was he
    Of famous London town.

John Gilpin's spouse said to her dear:
    'Though wedded we have been
These twice ten tedious years, yet we
    No holiday have seen.

'To-morrow is our wedding-day,
    And we will then repair
Unto the Bell at Edmonton,
    All in a chaise and pair.

'My sister, and my sister's child,
    Myself, and children three,
  Will fill the chaise; so you must ride
    On horseback after we.'

3

He soon replied: 'I do admire
Of womankind but one,
And you are she, my dearest dear,
Therefore it shall be done.

'I am a linen-draper bold,
    As all the world doth know,
And my good friend the calender
    Will lend his horse to go.'

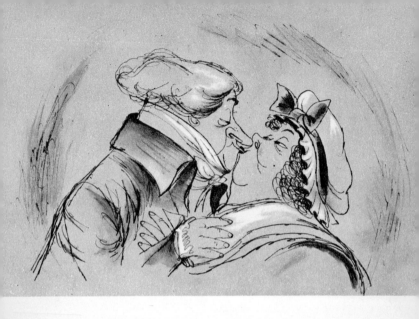

Quoth Mrs Gilpin: 'That's well said;
   And for that wine is dear,
We will be furnished with our own,
   Which is both bright and clear.'

John Gilpin kissed his loving wife;
   O'erjoyed was he to find,
That though on pleasure she was bent,
   She had a frugal mind.

The morning came, the chaise was brought,
   But yet was not allowed
To drive up to the door, lest all
   Should say that she was proud.

So three doors off the chaise was stayed,
   Where they did all get in;
Six precious souls, and all agog
   To dash through thick and thin.

Smack went the whip, round went the wheels,
  Were never folk so glad,
The stones did rattle underneath,
  As if Cheapside were mad.

John Gilpin at his horse's side
   Seized fast the flowing mane,
And up he got, in haste to ride,
   But soon came down again;

9

For saddle-tree scarce reached had he
    His journey to begin,
When, turning round his head, he saw
    Three customers come in.

So down he came; for loss of time
    Although it grieved him sore,
Yet loss of pence, full well he knew,
    Would trouble him much more.

'Twas long before the customers
    Were suited to their mind,
When Betty screaming came down stairs:
    'The wine is left behind!'

'Good lack!' quoth he, 'yet bring it me,
  My leathern belt likewise,
In which I bear my trusty sword,
  When I do exercise.'

Now Mistress Gilpin (careful soul!)
  Had two stone bottles found,
To hold the liquor that she loved,
  And keep it safe and sound.

Each bottle had a curling ear,
    Through which the belt he drew,
And hung a bottle on each side,
    To make his balance true.

Then over all, that he might be
    Equipped from top to toe,
His long red cloak, well brushed and neat,
    He manfully did throw.

13

Now see him mounted once again
　　Upon his nimble steed,
Full slowly pacing o'er the stones,
　　With caution and good heed.

But finding soon a smoother road
  Beneath his well-shod feet,
The snorting beast began to trot,
  Which galled him in his seat.

So, 'Fair and softly,' John he cried,
  But John he cried in vain;
That trot became a gallop soon,
  In spite of curb and rein.

So stooping down, as needs he must
  Who cannot sit upright,
He grasped the mane with both his hands,
  And eke with all his might.

His horse, who never in that sort
   Had handled been before,
What thing upon his back had got
   Did wonder more and more.

Away went Gilpin, neck or nought;
   Away went hat and wig;
He little dreamt, when he set out,
   Of running such a rig.

The wind did blow, the cloak did fly,
　　Like streamer long and gay,
Till, loop and button failing both,
　　At last it flew away.

Then might all people well discern
   The bottles he had slung;
A bottle swinging at each side,
   As hath been said or sung.

The dogs did bark, the children screamed,

Up flew the windows all;
And every soul cried out: 'Well done!'
As loud as he could bawl.

Away went Gilpin – who but he?
  His fame soon spread around;
'He carries weight!' 'He rides a race!'
  ''Tis for a thousand pound!'

And still, as fast as he drew near,
  'Twas wonderful to view,
How in a trice the turnpike-men
  Their gates wide open threw.

And now, as he went bowing down
   His reeking head full low,
The bottles twain behind his back
   Were shattered at a blow.

Down ran the wine into the road,
   Most piteous to be seen,
Which made his horse's flanks to smoke
   As they had basted been.

But still he seemed to carry weight,
   With leathern girdle braced;
For all might see the bottle necks
   Still dangling at his waist.

Thus all through merry Islington
   These gambols he did play,
Until he came unto the Wash
   Of Edmonton so gay;

And there he threw the Wash about
   On both sides of the way,
Just like unto a trundling mop,
   Or a wild goose at play.

At Edmonton his loving wife
   From the balcony spied
Her tender husband, wondering much
   To see how he did ride.

'Stop, stop, John Gilpin! Here's the house!'
   They all at once did cry;
'The dinner waits, and we are tired.'

Said Gilpin: 'So am I!'

But yet his horse was not a whit
    Inclined to tarry there!
For why? – his owner had a house
    Full ten miles off, at Ware.

So like an arrow swift he flew,
   Shot by an archer strong;
So did he fly – which brings me to
   The middle of my song.

Away went Gilpin, out of breath,
    And sore against his will,
Till at his friend the calender's
    His horse at last stood still.

The calender, amazed to see
    His neighbour in such trim,
Laid down his pipe, flew to the gate,
    And thus accosted him:

'What news? what news? your tidings tell;
  Tell me you must and shall –
Say why bareheaded you are come,
  Or why you come at all?'

Now Gilpin had a pleasant wit,
  And loved a timely joke;
And thus unto the calender
  In merry guise he spoke:

'I came because your horse would come,
  And, if I well forebode,
My hat and wig will soon be here
  They are upon the road.'

The calender, right glad to find
  His friend in merry pin,
Returned him not a single word,
  But to the house went in;

Whence straight he came with hat and wig;
    A wig that flowed behind,
A hat not much the worse for wear,
    Each comely in its kind.

He held them up, and in his turn
    Thus showed his ready wit,
'My head is twice as big as yours,
    They therefore needs must fit.

'But let me scrape the dirt away
    That hangs upon your face;
And stop and eat, for well you may
    Be in a hungry case.'

Said John : 'It is my wedding-day
    And all the world would stare,
If wife should dine at Edmonton,
    And I should dine at Ware.'

35

So, turning to his horse, he said,
  'I am in haste to dine;
'Twas for your pleasure you came here,
  You shall go back for mine.'

Ah, luckless speech, and bootless boast!
  For which he paid full dear;
For, while he spake, a braying ass
  Did sing most loud and clear:

Whereat his horse did snort, as he
    Had heard a lion roar,
And galloped off with all his might,
    As he had done before.

Away went Gilpin, and away
   Went Gilpin's hat and wig:
He lost them sooner than at first;
   For why? – they were too big.

Now Mistress Gilpin, when she saw
   Her husband posting down
Into the country far away,
   She pulled out half a crown;

And thus unto the youth she said
   That drove them to the Bell,
'This shall be yours, when you bring back
   My husband safe and well.'

The youth did ride, and soon did meet
   John coming back amain,
Whom in a trice he tried to stop
   By catching at his rein;

But not performing what he meant,
   And gladly would have done,
The frighted steed he frighted more,
   And made him faster run.

Away went Gilpin, and away
    Went postboy at his heels,
The postboy's horse right glad to miss
    The lumbering of the wheels.

Six gentlemen upon the road
    Thus seeing Gilpin fly,
With postboy scampering in the rear,
    They raised the hue and cry:

'Stop thief! stop thief! – a highwayman!'
 Not one of them was mute;
And all and each that passed that way
 Did join in the pursuit.

And now the turnpike gates again
 Flew open in short space;
The toll-men thinking, as before,
 That Gilpin rode a race.

And so he did, and won it too,
 For he got first to town;
Nor stopped till where he had got up
 He did again get down.

Now let us sing: Long live the king!
 And Gilpin, long live he!
And when he next doth ride abroad
 May I be there to see!